7/12

Painting

Sue Nicholson

QEB Publishing, Inc.

Published in the United States by
QEB Publishing, Inc.
23062 La Cadena Drive
Laguna Hills, CA 92653

www.qeb-publishing.com

Library of Congress Control Number: 2005921168

ISBN 1-59566-084-4

Written by Sue Nicholson
Designed by Susi Martin
Editor Paul Manning

Publisher Steve Evans
Creative Director Louise Morley
Editorial Manager Jean Coppendale

Printed and bound in China

The author and publisher would like to thank
Amy and Kane
Sarah Morley for making the models

Printed and bound in China

Note to teachers and parents

The projects in this book are aimed at children in grades
1 to 3 and are presented in order of difficulty, from easy
to more challenging. Each can be used as a separate
activity or as part of another area of study.

While the ideas in the book are offered as inspiration,
children should always be encouraged to draw from
their own imagination and first-hand observations.

All projects in this book require adult supervision.

Sourcing ideas

★ Encourage the children to source ideas from their
   own experiences, as well as from books, magazines,
   the Internet, art galleries, or museums.
★ Prompt them to talk about different types of art they
   have seen at home or on vacation.

★ Use the "Click for Art!" boxes as a starting point for
   finding useful material on the Internet.*
★ Suggest that each child keeps a sketchbook of
   their ideas.

Evaluating work

★ Encourage the children to share their work and talk
   about their ideas and ways of working. What do they
   like best/least about it? If they did it again, what
   would they do differently?
★ Help the children to judge the originality of their work
   and to appreciate the different qualities in others'
   work. This will help them to value ways of working
   that are different from their own.
★ Encourage the children by displaying their work.

* Website information is correct at the time of going to
   press. However, the publishers cannot accept liability
   for information or links found on third-party websites.

Contents

Words in bold, **like this**, are explained in the Glossary on page 24.

Getting started

This book will show you all kinds of wonderful painting projects. Here are some of the things you will need to get started.

Top tip
Collect old jam jars to hold water to wash your brushes in.

Basic equipment
- Paper and poster paper
- **Poster**, **acrylic**, and **watercolor paints**
- Pencils and paintbrushes
- Safety scissors
- White school glue

You will also need some extra items, which are listed separately for each project.

Use a soft pencil to sketch outlines before you paint.

Use a thin brush for details and a thick brush to paint large areas.

Paper
Smooth typing or copier paper is good for most paints. You can also buy special watercolor paper that does not wrinkle when wet.

Brushes
Brushes come in all shapes and sizes and can be used for different effects. Soft brushes are good to use with watercolor paints. Brushes with stiff **bristles** are better with acrylics.

Acrylic paints

Poster paints

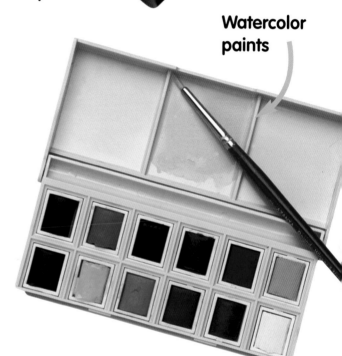

Watercolor paints

Paints

Poster paints are good for big, bold paintings. Use them straight from the jar or mix with water to make them thinner.

Acrylic paints are thick, bright, and easy to mix. Use them straight from the tube or mix with water.

Watercolor paints come in tubes or blocks. They are good for landscapes.

Mix your paints on a special **palette** or use an old white saucer or the lid of a plastic container or carton.

Top tip

Always carry a **sketchbook** for quick on-the-spot drawings. You can turn them into finished paintings later.

Mixing colors

All the different colors you can think of are made from just three primary colours: red, yellow, and blue.

Top tip

To make a color darker, don't just add black—try a different dark color.

To make a color lighter, add a little white paint.

Red **Yellow** **Blue**

Here's how the three primary colors can be used to mix other colors:

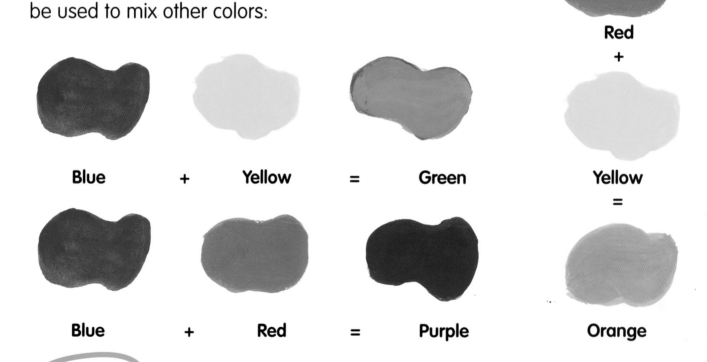

Blue + **Yellow** = **Green**

Blue + **Red** = **Purple**

Red
+
Yellow
=
Orange

Click for Art!

To see the vivid colors used by the French artist Gauguin, go to **www.ibiblio.org/wm/paint/auth/gauguin/** To find out more about color, visit **www.artlex.com** and click on "Color" in the "Shortcuts" panel on the left.

All the colors on the facing page can be shown on a color wheel.

Now try mixing some colors of your own. See how the colors change according to how much paint you use.

A lot of red and a little yellow gives this color:

A lot of yellow and a little red gives this color:

7

Fun with paint

You can paint with anything, from a twig to a toothbrush! See the box for things to try.

Paint effects

Painting tools

Try making a painting with:
- ★ an old toothbrush or sponge
- ★ scrunched-up rags or paper
- ★ a cotton swab
- ★ the edge of a piece of cardboard
- ★ the tip of a feather
- ★ a twig or flower stem
- ★ an old comb or plastic fork
- ★ your fingertips!

Flowing strokes painted with a feather tip

How many different paint effects can you make?

Try painting with different tools and materials, and test the effects on scratch paper. Label the results so you can remember which is which.

Paint effects using scrunched-up paper and fabric

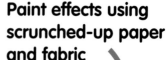

Paint dabbed on with a cotton ball for a soft, cloudy look

Scratchy pattern made by painting with a toothbrush

Click for Art!

To see an example of texture and movement in a painting, go to **www.moma.org** and search for "The Starry Night" by Vincent van Gogh.

Paint effects using thick cardboard

paint dragging

To make interesting patterns and **textures**, try dragging a comb or a twig through thick wet paint.

A comb with small pointed teeth gives a fine texture like cloth

A twig gives a rough texture like thick grass or tangled hair

9

Splitter splatter!

Make a lively painting by spattering paint onto paper with a brush or toothbrush.

You will need:
An old toothbrush

1 Draw fish and starfish outlines on a sheet of paper. Turn the paper over and place it face down on some newspaper.

2 Dip a toothbrush in yellow paint, then drag your finger over the bristles to spatter the paint on the paper. Try flicking yellow and orange paint with ordinary brushes, too.

3 Now flick blue and green paint onto a second sheet of paper. Use different shades of blue and green to make a speckled sea background.

Top tip
Paint spattering is messy! Wear a smock, and spread out plenty of newspaper to work on.

Follow the steps above to create this speckly underwater scene.

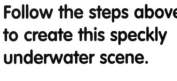

Click for Art! To see "drip paintings" by the American artist Jackson Pollock, go to **http://www.artlex.com/** and search for "Action painting."

4 When the paint is dry, turn the paper over and cut out the fish and starfish with safety scissors. Arrange them on your sea background and glue them down.

Desert landscape

1 Make cardboard **stencils** using the shapes below.

2 Arrange the stencils on a sheet of thick white paper. Use a small dab of glue to hold them in place.

Copy these shapes onto poster paper to create the desert landscape above.

3 Spatter yellow paint over the bottom part of the paper for the sand. Spatter blue paint above for the sky.

4 When the paint is dry, remove the cardboard stencils.

Straw paintings

Blowing paint through a straw makes the paint wander in wiggly lines and creates wonderful and unusual shapes.

A plastic drinking straw

1 Add water to some poster or acrylic paint to make the paint runny.

2 Drip a large blob of paint onto your paper with a brush.

Top tip
To mix colors, add a second color when the first is still wet. If you do not want your colors to mix, wait until the first color is dry before you add another.

3 Gently blow the paint through the straw. The paint will spread across the paper in wiggly lines.

4 Add different colors one by one. (See Top tip for hints on color mixing.)

5 Add details with a crayon or brush to complete your painting.

Sometimes a straw painting may start to look like something recognizable— such as a fluffy chick, a flower, a person's hair or an insect.

This straw painting was made into a tree by adding a trunk with a brush.

This chick's legs, eyes, and beak were added with pencil and orange crayon.

Click for Art! To explore paintings by Jackson Pollock, Mark Rothko, and Robert Rauschenberg, go to **www.sfmoma.org/anderson/** Click on "Start Project" and then "Explore 15 works."

Mirror paintings

By folding a painted piece of paper, you can make pictures that are **symmetrical** (the same on both sides).

You will need:

- A large sheet of white paper
- Soft pencil for sketching

1 Make a crease in your sheet of paper by folding it in half lengthwise, then opening it out again. Paint a band of green across the middle, just above the crease.

2 Paint in a pale blue sky. Dab the paint with a cotton ball to make white patches that look like clouds.

3 While the paint is still wet, fold the paper in half and press it down.

Top tip

Try other mirror art scenes, such as the sun setting over the ocean.

4 Leave the paper folded for a minute, then carefully open it out.

Click for Art!

To see an online gallery of children's art, go to **www.english.barnekunst.no/default.htm**

Brilliant butterfly

1 Fold a piece of white paper in half. On one side, paint half the body and the wings of a butterfly. Use thick paints and work quickly.

2 While the paint is still wet, fold the paper down the middle and press the white side onto the painted side.

3 Leave for a minute, then carefully peel open the paper.

5 Working quickly, paint a row of trees. Paint the trunks brown and dab on blobs of orange, red, and yellow for the leaves.

6 Fold the paper as before, then open it out. You should see a paler row of trees at the bottom of the page, looking like a reflection in a lake.

Dotty paintings

To blend colors, try using a pattern of different-colored dots and dashes.

You will need:
A paintbrush with a fine tip

Mixing colors

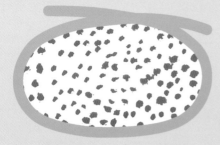

1 Before you begin your picture, practice making lots of tiny dots next to each other with the tip of your brush. Try one color first, such as red.

2 Now make some more red dots on a clean sheet of paper. This time, space the dots out a little.

3 When the red paint is dry, add yellow dots in between. Stand back. What color do the red and yellow dots look like from a distance?

4 Now try making dots and dashes with different colors and different-sized brushes.

Pink and turquoise dashes

Dark purple and lilac dots

Blue and red blobs

Frog on a lily pad

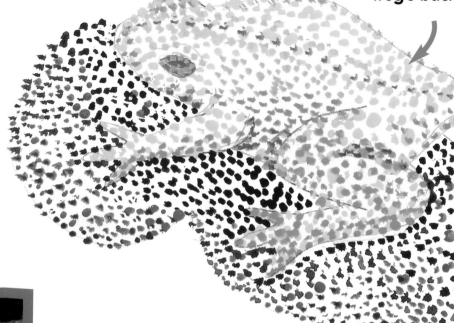

Yellow dots highlight the frog's back.

Top tip
Make darker dots and place them closer together to add detail and shading.

1 Plan your painting in your sketchbook or on a piece of scratch paper.

2 Lightly sketch the outline of your painting on a sheet of white paper.

3 Color each part of the picture with tiny dots of color. This dotty painting has dark green for the lily pads, pale green for the frog, and yellow and dark green dots for the frog's markings.

Click for Art!
To learn how the French painter Seurat made paintings out of tiny dots, go to **www.metmuseum.org/Works_of_Art/** and search for "Circus Sideshow."

Wax paintings

Use paint and wax crayons to make wax **resist** paintings. The wax resists the paint, so the color of the crayons shows through.

❶ Cover the bottom of your paper with a white crayon for snow.

You will need:
- Thick paper or poster paper
- Wax crayons
- Blue watercolor or poster paint

❷ Still using crayons, add a snowman in the middle. Give him an orange carrot nose, two eyes, a black hat, some buttons, and a striped scarf.

❸ Add white crayon dots for falling snow.

❹ Mix dark blue paint for the background. If you are using poster paint, add water to make it thinner.

Scraper effects

1 With wax crayons, create patches of bright color on thick paper.

Top tip

If you are making a scraper picture, be sure to use thick paper or cardboard, as ordinary paper may tear.

2 Paint three layers of black, dark blue, or purple acrylic paint over the crayon patches.

3 When the paint is dry, scrape a picture into the paint with a knitting needle. The bright colors will show through.

Lost in space!

To make this picture, draw the rocket, planets, and stars first using bright crayons. Then add black watercolor paint on top.

5 Brush the blue paint over your drawing. The crayon marks will resist the paint, so your drawing stands out.

Water paintings

Enjoy experimenting with watercolor paints. They are great for seas and skies!

You will need:

- Watercolor paper
- Watercolor paints
- A wide brush
- A thin, pointed brush
- A sponge, tissue paper or cotton balls

3 Paint the sea using shorter brushstrokes. Use orange, yellow, and blue. Let the colors run a little.

1 With a brush, paint clean water all over your sheet of watercolor paper.

2 Paint yellow stripes over the top half of your paper. Add orange stripes halfway down.

Top tip

To help the colors in the sea run together, drip a few drops of clean water over the paint.

4 While the paint is still wet, dab a cotton ball on the yellow sky so the patches look like pale clouds.

5 When the paint is dry, paint a black island and a palm tree. If you want, add a shark's fin pointing out of the water!

Watery skies

For cloudy skies, paint overlapping stripes of blue watercolor paint across your paper. Before the paint dries, dab it with a clean sponge. This will leave white patches that look like clouds.

These clouds were made by painting stripes of blue across wet paper, then dabbing the paint with scrunched-up tissue paper.

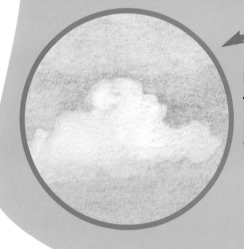

For a different effect, let the blue paint dry, then paint clouds in white watercolor paint.

Click for Art!

To see watercolors by the English artist Turner, go to **www.j-m-w-turner.co.uk/** Click on "Turner in Venice," scroll down, then click on the small pictures.

Special effects

Make your paintings special by adding glitter or cornstarch to paint, or sprinkling salt onto wet paint.

You will need:
- Glitter
- Cornstarch
- Soft, wide brush
- Salt crystals

1 Wet the paper all over with a soft, wide brush.

2 While the paper is wet, drip blobs of paint in a circle and let them spread.

3 Add a tiny dot of paint for the center of each flower. Sprinkle grains of salt over the painted petals. Watch how the salt soaks up the paint and makes speckled marks on the paper.

Flower painting

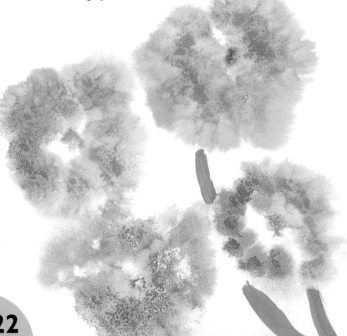

When the paint is dry, add stems for the flowers with a thin brush

Top tip
Shake off the salt when the paint is dry, or leave it on if you want more texture in your painting.

Click for Art!

For a good general children's art website including art galleries, art quizzes and information about artists and their work, visit **www.scribbleskidsart.com**

All that glitters

It's easy to make your own sparkly glitter paint. Just add glitter to acrylic or poster paint and paint it on with a brush as usual.

Adding texture

To thicken poster paint, add a few spoonfuls of cornstarch. Keep mixing until you have the texture you want. Paint with a brush as usual. If you like, make patterns in the paint with a stick or comb (see page 9).

23

Glossary

acrylic paint easy-to-mix paint that dries quickly and can be cleaned with soap and water

bristles fibers on the end of a paintbrush made of animal hair or nylon

palette a flat piece of wood or plastic used by artists to mix paints

poster paint thick paint that can be mixed with water

resist a substance such as wax that protects a surface so it does not get colored with paint or dye

sketchbook a small, easy-to-carry book for quick drawings and designs

stencil a shape cut out of cardboard which you can paint or print through or around

symmetrical a shape that is the same on both sides

texture the surface or "feel" of something: for example, fabric can be rough, soft, furry, or velvety

watercolor paint paint sold in tubes or as small solid blocks